July

Julie Murray

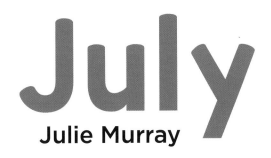

Abdo
MONTHS
Kids

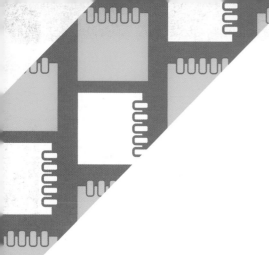

abdopublishing.com

Published by Abdo Kids, a division of ABDO, PO Box 398166, Minneapolis, Minnesota 55439.
Copyright © 2018 by Abdo Consulting Group, Inc. International copyrights reserved in all countries.
No part of this book may be reproduced in any form without written permission from the publisher.

Printed in the United States of America, North Mankato, Minnesota.

052017

092017

Photo Credits: Alamy, Glow Images, iStock, Shutterstock, ©Simon Davis/DFID p.23 / CC-BY 2.0

Production Contributors: Teddy Borth, Jennie Forsberg, Grace Hansen

Design Contributors: Christina Doffing, Candice Keimig, Dorothy Toth

Publisher's Cataloging in Publication Data

Names: Murray, Julie, 1969-, author.

Title: July / by Julie Murray.

Description: Minneapolis, Minnesota : Abdo Kids, 2018 | Series: Months |
     Includes bibliographical references and index.

Identifiers: LCCN 2016962342 | ISBN 9781532100215 (lib. bdg.) |
     ISBN 9781532100901 (ebook) | ISBN 9781532101458 (Read-to-me ebook)

Subjects: LCSH: July (Month)--Juvenile literature. | Calendar--Juvenile literature.

Classification: DDC 398/.33--dc23

LC record available at http://lccn.loc.gov/2016962342

Table of Contents

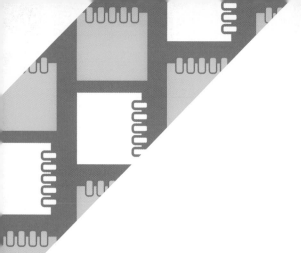

July

There are 12 months
in the year.

January

February

March

April

May

June

July

August

September

October

November

December

5

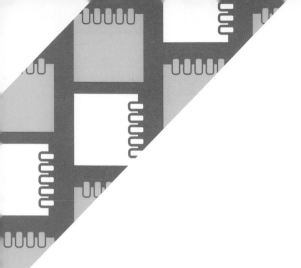

July is the 7th month.

It has 31 days.

July

1	2	3	4	5	6	7
8	9	10	11	12	13	14
15	16	17	18	19	20	21
22	23	24	25	26	27	28
29	30	31				

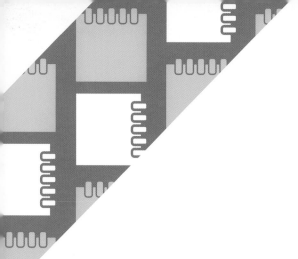

Boom! Boom! Rina watches fireworks. It is the 4th of July.

Malala Yousafzai was born in July. Her birthday is on the 12th.

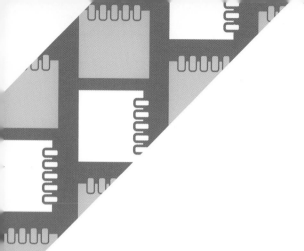

July can be hot! Maci cools off.

She eats ice cream.

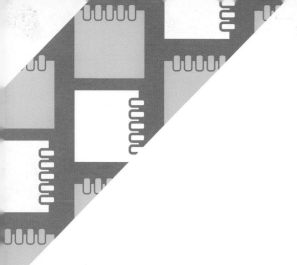

Joel goes camping.

He sleeps in a tent.

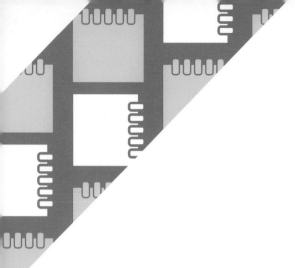

Kate goes swimming. She has fun in the pool.

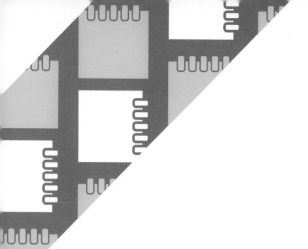

Eddy plays baseball.

His team wins!

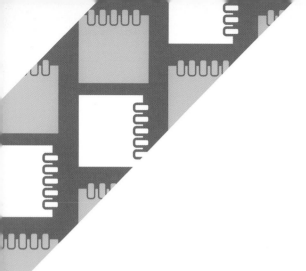

Milo's family has a picnic.

They love July!

Fun Days in July

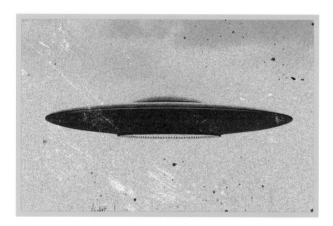

World UFO Day
July 2

National Fried Chicken Day
July 6

Amelia Earhart Day
July 24

International Tiger Day
July 29

Glossary

4th of July
Also called Independence Day, a day that celebrates the adoption of the Declaration of Independence in 1776.

Malala Yousafzai
a Pakistani and activist for education for all children, and the youngest person to receive a Nobel Peace Prize.

Index

abdokids.com

Use this code to log on to abdokids.com and access crafts, games, videos, and more!

Abdo Kids Code:
MJK0215